WORDs aRe MY SUPERPOWER

WORDS ARE MY SUPERPOWER

A Kid's Guide to Affirmations, Mantras, and Positive Thinking

Harold Green III

Illustrated by
ANDREA PIPPINS

RP|KIDS
PHILADELPHIA

Running Press Kids
Hachette Book Group
1290 Avenue of the Americas, New York, NY 10104
www.runningpress.com/rpkids
@runningpresskids

Distributed in the United Kingdom by Little, Brown Book Group UK,
Carmelite House, 50 Victoria Embankment, London, EC4Y 0DZ

First Edition: July 2024

Published by Running Press Kids, an imprint of Hachette Book Group, Inc. The Running Press
Kids name and logo are trademarks of Hachette Book Group, Inc.

Running Press books may be purchased in bulk for business, educational, or promotional
use. For more information, please contact your local bookseller or the Hachette Book Group
Special Markets Department at Special.Markets@hbgusa.com.

The publisher is not responsible for websites (or their content)
that are not owned by the publisher.

Print book cover and interior design by Frances J. Soo Ping Chow.

Library of Congress Cataloging-in-Publication Data
Names: Green, Harold, III, author. | Pippins, Andrea, illustrator,
Title: Words are my superpower : a kid's guide to affirmations, mantras,
and positive thinking / Harold Green III ; illustrated by Andrea Pippins.
Description: First Edition. | Philadelphia : Running Press, 2024.
| Audience: Ages 8–13 | Audience: Grades 4–6 |
Identifiers: LCCN 2023045203 | ISBN 9780762481590 (hardcover) |
ISBN 9780762481606 (ebook)
Subjects: LCSH: Thought and thinking—Juvenile literature. | Affirmations—Juvenile
literature. | Mantras—Juvenile literature. | Interpersonal communication—Juvenile literature.
Classification: LCC BF441 .G734 2024 | DDC 153.4/2—dc23/eng/20231117
LC record available at https://lccn.loc.gov/2023045203

ISBNs: 978-0-7624-8159-0 (trade paperback), 978-0-7624-8160-6 (ebook)

Printed in China

APS

10 9 8 7 6 5 4 3 2 1

ThiS bOOk iS dediCated tO
the kid in all Of US, Still trying
tO find the right WOrdS.

HG

CONTENTS

Introduction IX

HUG
TIRED
HUNGRY
ANXIETY
COURAGE
SADNESS
FEAR
CONFIDENCE
AFFIRMATIONS

INTRODUCTION

Have you ever heard someone say "Use your words?" From the time we begin to speak, we are taught to use our words to help us communicate what we're feeling, like "I'm tired" or "I'm hungry," or to ask for what we want ("I need a hug" or "I want my toy"). As we get older, the power and responsibility that comes with "using your words" only grows. Words offer protection and encouragement and serve as a reminder of how amazing you are. You can use your words to help you battle all the villains life throws your way. By villains, I don't necessarily mean people. A villain can be any obstacle—sadness, anxiety or fear, and self-doubt—that tries to hold you back from your fullest potential. But words can help us conquer all those foes because words are more powerful than we often realize. Keep in mind, not every battle is with an external foe; sometimes, we have battles within ourselves. Words help us expand upon those internal conflicts or the expression of ourselves. I want you to think of certain categories of words as superheroes and see how the words themselves give you superpowers to overcome what stands in the way.

So, in this book I want to introduce you to how affirmations can give you "power-ups," the way compliments can give you confidence, and how mantras can slow down time. Did you know optimism can make you feel strong? Or, that empathy can turn you into a safe space? I want to show you that gratitude can change your heart.

It's important to remember, however, that even superheroes can become supervillains if their powers are used improperly. Have you ever heard words used to hurt people's feelings or to make others feel like they don't belong? That is an example of words turning into villains. We must be very aware of how we use our words and why we call upon them. One of the golden rules in life is that if you don't have anything nice to say, then you say nothing at all, but I believe that it should be added that if you HAVE something nice to say, then you should say it. We can use words to bring a smile to someone's face, laughter to a room, or to ease our pain when we are sad or scared, and *that* is part of what makes words so powerful.

  I have built a very strong relationship with words over the course of my life. It's a relationship I find great value in. I have watched words bring people together, tear people apart, and call them to action. As human beings, our ability to communicate through written, verbal, and visual language sets us apart from other animals. It makes us unique, *but* it can also make life complicated if we forget to use our words to create beauty in this world.

━━━━━━

You are going to feel a lot of things in life, and I hope that this book gives you the courage and the tools to talk about those feelings in a productive way; not just with others but in the conversations that you have with yourself. No, talking to yourself is not silly; and, yes, how you talk to yourself is important, too. Honestly, the conversations that we have with ourselves sometimes shape the way we talk to others, so be sure to find kind words for yourself as well. I truly hope by the end of this book you find the beautiful power in words and in yourself.

versus

Freedom
or Fear

I once ran from the things that scared me—

until I realized there was no finish line.

Once I dared to face the things that scared me,

that is when I freed my mind.

ONE OF THE MOST AMAZING THINGS

about words is that they have the power to help us face our fears—and fear comes in all forms. Maybe you are afraid of spiders, or you have a fear of swimming, or even roller coasters! For some of us, fear can be more internal. Some of us have a fear of public speaking, or a fear of failing that causes us to not even try certain things. Fear looks different for all of us, but what is empowering is being able to communicate your feelings.

How we use words to describe new experiences or situations can immediately change our perception of what's in front of us. For example, let's imagine that you are going on a trip but have never flown in a plane before. Despite your excitement about the trip, you can't help but feel nervous about the flight, and that fear is overshadowing everything else. Instead of focusing on how scared you are, tell yourself how beautiful the view will be or how nice it will be to get juice and cookies from the flight attendants. Just changing how you speak or think about situations that scare you can change how you feel about them.

Have you ever attended a new school? How did you feel on that first day? What were you telling yourself before you arrived? Maybe you said or thought things like "I don't want to go to a new school," "I won't know anyone," or "What if the teachers are mean?" It's easy to approach a situation like that with anger or fear, but in doing so, you close yourself off from the beauty of new experiences. You can just as easily replace those thoughts with "I am so excited to experience a new school," "I get to make new friends," or "I wonder what new things I will learn from my new teachers." This approach creates a mindset of excitement and openness.

Sometimes we fear other people because of what we have been told about them, so we have ideas about them before even meeting. There are times when

that happens toward a whole group of people. For instance, as an African American male in this country, I often deal with the fear that I will be prejudged because of my skin color. There have been times that I could see people become visibly more comfortable after hearing me talk, and I wished that their predetermined thoughts of me didn't create a tense situation. I try to keep those types of things in mind when I am dealing with new people. I try to think about how I've been made to feel before.

We can fear people because of how they look. There are people who don't smile often, or they wear religious garb, or they are physically bigger than you. After the terrorist attacks of September 11, 2001, many Muslims were wrongfully profiled because of their religious affiliations. They still deal with the effects of that moment today. Muslim women wearing hijabs were harassed and Muslim men were wrongfully labeled as terrorists. It's an unfortunate but all too true example of how fear can change how we interact with people. What we have heard about groups of people, and individuals, can change how we treat them.

Mislabeling happens in so many ways. Think about the kid who is labeled "bad" but may just be misguided or seeking love and attention. Or the young lady who gets called mean names for the types of clothes she wears, when that may just be what she is comfortable in and how she chooses to express her individuality. What about the kid who's called a nerd but is just studious and passionate about learning? These labels can damage relationships and people's self-esteem. You have to remember: We are just human beings with different ways of existing, but if we reconsider the words we use when talking about other people, we have the ability to break cycles of fear and judgment.

We may fear people because of an interaction we had with them on a bad day, and we assume that is who they always are. We may call someone rude, but they may just be shy; boring when they are actually quiet or thoughtful; aggressive when, in reality, they are just passionate. In most of these cases, using our words to get to know people can change those perceptions we have. I am not telling you that you will become best friends with everyone, but there is a good chance that with every conversation you are willing to have, the more you will decrease the fear, anxiety, and awkwardness that comes with new encounters. Your classmate who always has headphones in and does not talk much may not be as intimidating as you once thought. Maybe no one has taken the time to really get to know them. They may have a fear of meeting new people. Maybe all

it will take to break down the wall is a simple smile from you or asking them what they're listening to. We can't relate to where someone else is coming from if we don't take the time to consider they might also be going through something.

Fear is an emotion, which means it is not permanent, but what *can* have a lasting effect is your ability to use words to help you deal with fear. Being intentional about the words you use helps reframe your approach and response to pretty much everything. You must continue to use your words in a way that helps you defeat fear. You cannot do it one time and think that will magically help you overcome a fear you may have. You have to practice being more mindful in how you use your words.

Fear will try to get the best of you if you don't have the proper tools to face it, and your words are one of your best tools to conquer fear.

super thoughts

What was the last thing that scared you, and how did you deal with it?

When have you faced a fear head-on? How did you feel after?

Has fear ever held you back from an experience?

Almighty Affirmations

The thoughts I think are true.

The words I say, I do.

My mind is powerful.

So, that means I am too.

When I speak to myself,

I speak with the love I know.

I keep an open mind—

to give myself room to grow.

ALMIGHTY AFFIRMATION

This brings us to the first superhero I want to introduce you to—the Almighty Affirmation. Affirmation has the power to change your day, prepare you for hardships, and present you with power-ups that allow you to conquer any stage of life that you must face. Affirmation's superpower is mind control because it changes the way you think. Some super-heroes are called on for life's big battles, but Affirmation is an available superhero who you can call on throughout the day.

An affirmation can be any positive saying that you use to control how you see your reality. For example, if something scares you, remind yourself, "I am stronger than the things that make me feel weak." If you have goals that you want to accomplish, then tell yourself, "Everything that I want to do, I will do at a high level!" If you are unsure of yourself, then say, "I only know how to believe in myself." Affirmations can be used in so many situations when you need support.

There are times when I feel less than, or in need of help, and I have to call on Affirmation to help me move forward or to change my outlook. I want you

13

to think about the times in your life when someone told you how great of a job you did, or how proud of you they were. Think about how that made you feel. Did you feel like you grew a few inches? Did you feel more confident doing that same thing the next time? Did your mood instantly improve? Now, I want you to think about how wonderful it would be to create that feeling whenever you need. That's what affirmations have the power to do.

Whenever you feel like you can't do something, or you aren't good at something, I want you to tell yourself, "My best effort will offer me the best results." That's an important affirmation because it gives you room to be patient with yourself. If you are willing to give your best effort, then you are willing to accept that is what will give you the best results. Expecting someone else's results from your best effort is unrealistic and can damage our self-confidence. Did you score as high as someone else on a test? Did you score as many points in the game as they did? Did you read as many books? Comparing ourselves, or being compared by others, becomes a trap. But here's where affirmations can help! The more you tell yourself that your best is not only enough, but enough for *you*, the harder it will be for the world to tear you down with their comparisons. We must be willing to do our best and accept our best. Be proud of yourself when you know you've done all you can do.

You also must remember that the best you gave today is not necessarily the best you can give tomorrow. Affirmations give you room to grow. If you keep practicing, or keep studying, or keep trying, then your best keeps getting better, as do the results, and so the only thing you need to compare it to is your last best effort.

Have you ever been in a situation where you didn't feel liked, or maybe even loved? It could be something like the kids at school being mean to you, or even someone at home. No one is going to be liked by everyone. That is just how life and human nature work, but if *you* know that you are likable and lovable, then that is what really matters at the end of the day. And, realistically, that doesn't take away the sting of the actions of others, but how you feel about yourself can truly help you navigate the tough times. So, every day you should tell yourself, "I am the love I want to see in the world. Wherever I go, I bring love with me."

When we don't feel liked or loved, we may find ourselves willing to do things we think will make people like or love us; and, sometimes, that willingness and desperation for approval makes it easier for people to take advantage of us or present us with fleeting feelings. By fleeting feelings, I mean they like or love us in the immediate, or because of what we are doing for them in the moment, but those feelings don't last long. If we think buying someone candy will make them like us, then we do that, but once the candy runs out, so do they. If we think that making fun of other people will help us fit in, then we do that; and once that is no longer the "cool" thing, then we lose those "friends" we thought we had. Not to mention you've hurt someone else just to impress others. It's never worth it.

But, if you tell yourself every day that *you* are the love that you wish to see in this world, then you don't have to go far to fill that space within that looks for love and kindness. As human beings, feeling loved and cared for is important for our development; unfortunately, however, we are not all given the same amount of nurturing and kindness. That is why it's up to us to make sure we feel that love.

You are more than enough. You are likable. There are so many people in this world who will feel that way about you, and it makes it so much easier to find those people when you feel that way about yourself. So, remind yourself every morning that you are love and that you don't have to go out searching for it.

Affirmations also can turn goals into reality. Let's say that your grades weren't what you wanted them to be, and you knew you could earn better ones. Well, every day that you go to school you should be telling yourself, "I am a hard worker, because I choose to be." Affirmations aren't magic. Saying these words won't cast a spell on your teachers and cause them to magically change your grades. Affirmations are words that empower you, that make you believe. That belief must be followed by action. Affirmations just remind you who you are and what you are capable of; it is up to you to put in the actual work to make your goals a reality.

Being a writer has created a lot of opportunities for me in life, and one of my daily affirmations is "Thank you for the opportunities I am presented with." I say thank you before opportunities even present themselves because I know if I keep working hard at what I do, then the opportunities are sure to follow, but it takes work, and the work starts with a positive mentality.

There are so many times in life that we wait on people to affirm or acknowledge us, but I want you to know you don't have to wait for someone to tell you that you did a good job. You don't have to wait for someone to tell you that you are beautiful. You don't have to wait for someone to tell you that you are smart. You don't have to wait for someone to tell you that you can change the world. Sure, it's nice to hear those things from people, but if we wait to hear those wonderful things from others before we can believe them about ourselves, then we may be waiting longer than we think. So, make a habit of telling yourself the things you have been waiting to hear.

When you wake up, you should say an affirmation. When you arrive at school, say an affirmation. When you get nervous before a test, say an affirmation. When you are headed home, say an affirmation. When you are about to drift off to sleep—you guessed it—say an affirmation.

How we talk to ourselves is just as important as how we talk to others, and if you are used to being kind to yourself and encouraging, then you will be that same way with others. Be your best self to get your best results; be love and give love; speak your goals into existence while working to make them happen.

CHALLENGE YOURSELF TO USE THESE WORDS TO CREATE
TEN SEPARATE AFFIRMATIONS FOR YOURSELF!

1. Accomplish
2. Beautiful
3. Believe
4. Can
5. Capable

6. Excellent
7. Happy
8. Healthy
9. Increase
10. Prepared

Finish this sentence: "I am at my best when I _____."

Who affirms you the most in life?

WO

INSECU

rds versus

RITIES

me > insecurities

One day

I just decided that I was enough.

I didn't make an announcement,

or throw a party.

I just decided

to make peace

with the things

that wanted me in pieces.

INSECURITIES ARE RELENTLESS. THEY HAVE A WAY OF SHOWING UP

when they were not invited to the party. You can get all dressed up in a new outfit and fresh shoes, and here comes an insecurity making you feel less than. You can study hard for a test and right before the test is to be handed out, here comes an insecurity making you doubt yourself. You can be around a group of peers, having a good time, and suddenly—boom!—an insecurity makes you feel like you do not belong.

We all have dealt with insecurities in some form or fashion. The difference is *how* we deal with them. Do you let insecurities define you, or do you define the amount of power your insecurities have over you?

I previously told you how powerful affirmations are when used daily, but they are also very helpful when dealing with insecurities. Obviously, insecurities can pop up at random times, so saying an affirmation in the moment may be too late, but if you make affirmations a part of your daily routine, then it is harder for insecurities to show up continuously.

For example, let's say that you are insecure about your skin color because you have been made to feel like it is unattractive. If you start your day by saying "I am beautiful inside and out. My skin reflects that," then it becomes harder for your insecurity to just pop up on you because you have already declared how you feel about the thing trying to make you feel bad. Words are not a cure-all for your insecurity, but they equip you to deal with the uncomfortable moments that insecurities can create.

Here is another example: What if you have an insecurity about how much money your family has? Maybe you do not feel as if you have as much as others around you. If you constantly used the affirmation "I have all that I need, and all that I want is on the way," then that insecurity has very little room to show up and take over because you have assured yourself of who you are and what you have.

So many insecurities develop from comparing ourselves to others and never being told that we are more than enough. Think about how any of your insecurities formed. They most likely started from words used to put you down. If you are told you aren't as smart as a classmate, you may start questioning your intelligence. If you are told you are not as attractive as someone else, you may start questioning your looks. If you are told you are not as talented as someone else, you may question what you are capable of.

You were not born with insecurities. Insecurities are often triggered by words that find spaces in your mind where love, confidence, and bravery do not exist. So, if the wrong words can cause you to have insecurities, then, naturally, the right words can protect you from them. If you do not have people in your life who

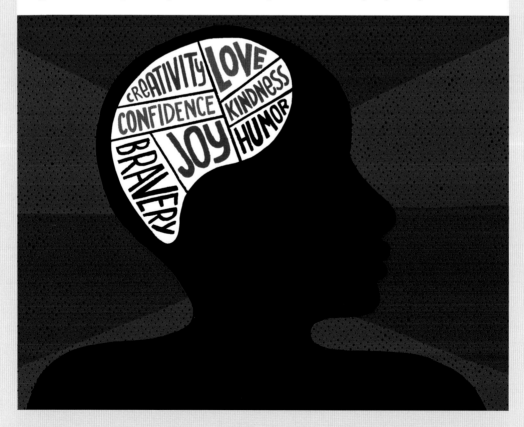

affirm you on a regular basis, then the best way to defeat a negative mindset is by using positive words when talking or thinking about yourself—words that will help challenge insecurities. Instead of thinking of yourself as emotional, you can say, "I'm in tune with my feelings." If you are made to feel insecure about your financial status, you can think of yourself as rich in love or friendship. If you are insecure about your clothing, you can think of it as having your own style. It's all about perspective!

Think of your mind like an apartment building. People who live in apartment buildings are called tenants and people who manage apartment buildings are called landlords. You are the landlord of your mind, so fill that apartment building mind of yours with love, confidence, and bravery, and you will see a change in how your mind works.

Investigating Your Insecurities

- What are some of your biggest insecurities, and when did they start?
- Do your insecurities stop you from going after things you want?
- Have you ever overcome an insecurity?
- If you could magically delete one insecurity, what would it be?

The case for compliments

The way you shine

Helps me see the light in me.

I am a reflection.

You are a mirror for me.

If I was granted a wish

it would be that these words

bring you bliss.

CONFIDENT COMPLIMENT

The second superhero I would like to introduce you to is the Confident Compliment. Its superpower, as its name suggests, is confidence. When you give someone a compliment, you begin building a connection with the person to whom you're speaking. Taking time to compliment people also has the power to make you (and others) feel more comfortable in otherwise uncomfortable spaces.

Have you ever walked into a room and felt like you were the only one there, even though the room was full? Or have you felt anxious because it seemed like everyone was looking at you? What if I told you compliments could help you in those situations?

Compliments can change the entire energy of a situation. While you are in that room we imagined earlier, if you choose one person and compliment them, whether it be about something they are wearing or how they carry themselves, just watch how it can change your connection to the room and, in turn, your

confidence. Everyone does not react to compliments the same, but when you are genuine about what you are saying, it can help break down barriers and build connections.

Finding special things about people and pointing them out makes even the hardest-to-reach individuals feel good. It is nice to feel seen. It also feels good to see people. We often spend a lot of time in our own bubbles and don't take the time to see what makes people special or stand out.

If you like the way someone dresses, you can tell them, "I love your style! It's so unique." Suppose someone has a great smile; you can say, "I think your smile is awesome. It really lights up the room." Or maybe there is someone in your life you enjoy talking to; tell them, "I enjoy the things we talk about. I think they are so interesting." One of my favorites is when people are funny! You can tell them that they have a great sense of humor and they always make you laugh. Some of these compliments may feel obvious, but you'd be surprised at how often we don't tell people the things we appreciate or enjoy about them. And more importantly, people often aren't told nice things about themselves, even the "simple" things.

Compliments also have the power to give you confidence in situations where you may be lacking it. If you are meeting new people for the first time, that can be intimidating; but you can control the situation with compliments. Imagine someone is being mean to you (because, sometimes, immature people do this when new people enter their space). You can disarm them and de-escalate the situation with a compliment. Now they have two choices, they can either double down on their meanness or realize that you are not there to threaten them. Either way, you now have the upper hand.

By the same token, complimenting people can leave you vulnerable. You can compliment someone who does not compliment you back, or, even worse, who says something mean to you in return. What do you do then? You do not let it change you. The point of offering compliments is not to get one back. The point is to be a light in this world and to illuminate every space you walk in. It is hard to ignore the light.

One of my favorite things to do is compliment strangers and just go on with my day. You never know what someone is going through—perhaps they are having a tough day, or maybe they feel unseen—so taking the time to shine your light through your words can be a game changer. It makes me so happy to think I have the power to make a person feel better. To this day, I still remember compliments that I have received from complete strangers.

Superpowers are not always about what helps us defeat others; sometimes, superpowers are things that help others feel safe and protected. They can make people feel warm and secure from the meanness that this world can sometimes offer us.

Compliment Catalog

- You are an amazing friend!
- I learned something new from you. (Tell them what it was.)
- It's hard not to have a good time when you're around.
- You inspire me!
- You have great taste in music.
- I think you are so much fun.
- You are such a good listener.
- You are so brave.
- You are so calm. It makes me feel at ease.
- I admire how hard you work.

super thoughts

How do you feel after receiving compliments?

How do you feel after giving compliments?

WO

ANXI

rds

Breaking Boxes

Some spaces,

no matter how big,

feel like boxes.

Boxes lined with shrink wrap.

Sometimes, I feel like

I am shrinking.

When the walls close in,

I wish I could push back.

The times I remembered

how big I am

are the times
I got my
breath back.

HAVE YOU EVER FELT ANXIETY

before? How did it show up for you? What gives you anxiety? Is it new situations? Is it certain spaces? Is it memories? Is it certain types of people? What if I told you that words can help you with your anxiety? You would probably say, "Isn't that what you have been saying about everything in this whole book?" And I would say, "Yes, that's correct."

There are small things in our everyday mindset and communication that can truly help us deal with anxiety* or stop it before it even shows up. Sometimes anxiety pops up because we feel overwhelmed, but feeling overwhelmed or underprepared can often come down to a mindset. I want to tell you something that I have been doing with my sons since they could talk to help prevent anxiety.

I make them replace a simple word with a simple phrase so that their outlook on executing tasks, big or small, is optimistic. The word they are not allowed to say is "can't" and the phrase they have to replace it with is "I am having a hard time . . ." At first glance, that phrase may not seem much better, but it changes everything about the sentence and situation.

If one of my sons says, "I can't figure out this problem," that means they believe there is no chance for them to figure it out. The problem has defeated them.

"CAN'T"

gives the impression that you have no other options, which can make any situation feel hopeless and create anxiety around said task.

---

* Some forms of anxiety require medical assistance and there is no shame in asking for professional help. This is by no means a replacement for professional medical solutions.

But if one of my sons says, "I am having a hard time figuring out this problem," that means that the problem is difficult, but there is an opportunity to find a solution if you keep working at it. That minor substitution in word choice rewires your brain to always believe that you are capable, even if you must work a little harder. That little bit of optimism makes it more difficult for anxiety to creep in and make you feel powerless or overwhelmed.

Some people struggle with anxiety because they do not like what may be considered conflict. Sometimes conflict can be as simple as just telling someone "No." If you are someone who does not like conflict, communicating your feelings can be very uncomfortable. So, how do you use your words to help decrease anxiety in moments like that?

Let's say someone asks you to go to the park after school, but you were specifically told to wait out front to be picked up. Instead of saying "I don't think I should go to the park," use more definitive language like "I am not going to the park. I am going wait here for my ride, but thanks for the invite."

What is the difference? When you use a phrase such as, "I do not think . . ." it makes it sound as if you are not sure, and it leaves room for people to sway your thinking. Being direct won't just help you at school or at the park, it will help you all the way through your adult years. Uncomfortable conversations will always have the power to create anxiety, but remember that you have the power to control the conversation. The more you learn to use your words in this way, the less uncomfortable you will be and the less anxious you will feel.

Lastly, sometimes going certain places can give us anxiety if we have bad feelings attached to those places. Let's say that someone has been bullied at school, so most days just walking through those doors takes a whole lot of courage. This is where your affirmations and mantras can really help! If you create a habit of telling yourself affirmations before school, or if you have a mantra you can turn to whenever you need support, you can change your emotional attachment to the space you are in.

You have the power to build your own happiness. We all deserve safe spaces, and we all should know we have the power to create those safe spaces for ourselves as well.

I want you to close your eyes and say, "Happiness finds me when I feel lost," ten times. Now try that anytime you feel the need to. You can create your own version of it, but find a mantra that feels good to you and helps you find your happy place. Our brains are powerful machines and can be rewired, so be intentional in what you are saying to yourself. May your positivity leave no room for anxiety.

mega Mantras

Love.

Love.

Love.

Love.

Joy.

Joy.

Joy.

Joy.

Success.

Success.

Success.

Success.

Peace.

Peace.

Peace.

Peace.

The third superhero I would like to introduce you to is the Mega Mantra. Mantra's superpower is the ability to slow down time. Mantras are sounds, words, or phrases you repeat during meditation. And what is meditation? Meditation is the practice of stillness.

Mantras are like affirmations, but with a slightly different intention. While meditating, you can repeat a word or a phrase to help you clear your mind and focus. This is particularly helpful for those of us who have a hard time doing just that—clearing our mind and focusing.

Close your eyes and visualize your body—your organs, veins, muscles, and bones. In your mind, without speaking aloud, repeat the phrase "I am confident."

Picture the words flowing through your organs and filling up all those veins. Let the confidence flow through you. Picture the confidence filling up your organs:

- First, your heart so that the confidence can flow through your arteries and veins to the rest of your body.
- Next, direct the flow of the words to your brain, filling up every inch, leaving no room for doubt.
- Now, your stomach so that whenever you get those nervous butterflies in your gut, you remember your belly is full of confidence, too.
- Lastly, I want you to see the confidence filling your lungs so that you breathe and speak confidence.

Can I tell you something? Mantras are not easy for me because my mind is always racing, but being intentional about setting aside time to be more mindful makes it easier for me. It can be hard to sit still, but that is why I think mantras are so important—because we can call on them wherever we are, whatever we're doing, to help us focus on the things we want. You do not have to be in a dimly lit room with candles burning and nature sounds playing in the background. You can be among a crowd of people, in the shower, in a car, at lunch, in your bed, wherever you feel the need to center yourself. Sometimes, it seems like the world is moving too fast and we can feel overwhelmed. Mantras can help us center ourselves and pay attention to the things that are most important to us.

If you are an athlete and you get anxious before games, mantras are a great way to focus your mind and create a routine before games. For example, "I am

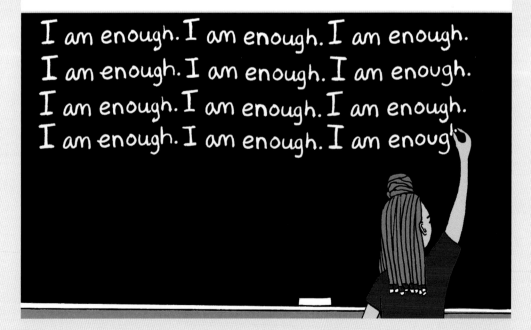

a champion" is a great one. Locate a space where you can be by yourself and repeat your mantra until you feel calm and prepared to take on the game.

Mantras work in all kinds of spaces. They can help any of us reset our minds. How amazing is that?! There were times while writing this book when I would repeat the mantra "This book will be helpful" before I started writing or while I was writing, and it helped me stay focused and keep my goals at the front of my mind.

There used to be a punishment in school where you would have to write whatever it was that the teacher felt you should not do anymore on the chalk-board repeatedly. So, if you threw paper in the classroom and the teacher caught you, then you would have to write on the chalkboard "I will not throw paper in the classroom" over and over until the teacher felt you had learned your lesson. Mantras are like that, but it is repeating something good over and over until you get it. So, clear your mind's chalkboard and write your mantra across it, repeatedly.

super thoughts

What is the first thing that comes to mind when you think of peace?

When does your mind feel the calmest?

What do you do when you feel like you can't concentrate?

CHALLENGE:
Create a list of three mantras you can use during stressful times.

rds versus

Mistakes
Don't make me

When I let the world down,

I learned to lift myself up.

Sometimes,

that is a lot of weight to carry.

But the more I lift,

the stronger I get.

And moving forward

doesn't look so scary.

HOW MANY MISTAKES

have you made this week? Be honest. I'll tell you a story about a mistake I made before that I learned from. I take pride in being on time, but I also enjoy naps when I can get them. One time, I had a meeting scheduled and had enough time to take a quick nap before it started. I thought I had set my alarm to two thirty PM, but it was actually set to two thirty AM! I woke up later than expected but was still able to make the meeting. Thankfully, those who I was meeting with were very understanding. Ever since then, I set two alarms and triple-check the time.

I gave myself grace in that moment, which helped me move forward with a better sense of self and my situation. I told myself that it was a simple mistake, and it didn't have unsurmountable consequences. I reminded myself of how grateful I felt that I was still able to make the meeting and how chill those on the other side were. We all make mistakes, but how we talk to ourselves during those mistakes makes a big difference.

Oftentimes we talk to ourselves the way we have been talked to. So, if you are used to being yelled at, criticized, or even called names just for making a mistake, then you are more likely to talk to yourself in that same regard. Do you tell yourself how "dumb" you are or "stupid" you are if you make a mistake? Please do not. You must present yourself with grace, even if you have not been given it by others. You owe yourself grace.

Mistakes will happen. Maybe you put the wrong answer on a test when you knew the right one. Maybe you accidentally made a bad play in a game and cost your team a point. Maybe you put your keys in a different place because you were distracted. Whatever the case may be, your mistake is most likely not the end of the world, and, instead of reacting as if it is, you must be graceful with yourself. Tell yourself it is okay. Remind yourself that you are worth more than your mistakes.

These may seem like simple things, but they can change a situation. Sometimes we spend too much time beating ourselves up for a mistake, which can lead to us making more mistakes in the moment or losing sight that the moment is still happening.

Forgiving ourselves helps us to find a clearer path forward. Being overly critical of ourselves clouds our vision. Just imagine you are in front of a group presenting and you say the wrong thing by mistake. Do you get caught up on that mistake, or do you tell yourself it is okay and continue to execute the presentation at a high level? And here's the thing: Not everyone is going to be as forgiving about your mistakes. And that is why it is up to you to create that soft landing for yourself. You cannot rely on the world to give you the grace you deserve.

Which brings me to my next point: You should absolutely give others the grace you give yourself. Everyone is going to make mistakes; walk into situations knowing that. You can let people know how their mistakes affected you without being nasty about it.

Be as graceful as you possibly can with your language. Your reaction to other peoples' mistakes may be more important than the mistake itself. One of the major themes of this book is human connection. I want to present you with the tools to be better human beings for yourselves and others. We never know what someone is going through, and the way we respond in our interactions with one another could make or break someone's day—or shape their perspective on the world.

The kid you do not know who accidentally stepped on your shoes may be going through more than you realize, and the fact that you kindly told them "It's okay" may help them through the day, or the school year. The world needs that gentleness. The world needs your grace.

SITUATION	GRACE
You and a former friend (who are no longer friends because they said mean things behind your back) are now partners for a project.	Tell them, "I have let go of any hard feelings I had because things happen. I hope that we can agree on that and do great work together."
You didn't make a team that you tried out for and now you feel bad.	Tell yourself, "I know I tried my hardest, but I will work even harder and try out again next time. This does not make me a failure."
A new student has just arrived at your school and seems to be painfully shy.	Consider approaching them to say, "I know it's hard making friends in a new place, so I'm down to show you around. If that's okay with you."

Useful Phrases for Mistakes

- I'm sorry that I _____.
- I apologize for _____.
- It was not my intention to _____.
- I didn't mean any harm.
- If there is anything I can do to fix this, please let me know.

super thoughts

When is the last time you made a mistake?
Was it a big mistake, or a small one?

—

Have you ever made a mistake
that you thought was unfixable?

—

Does making a mistake ever keep you
from doing things?

—

How do you react when other people
make mistakes?

optimism is always in season

They called me naïve

because when autumn came

all they saw were leaves,

but I saw trees

willing to shed the old

to make room for the new.

It is so easy to lose hope

if you only focus on the now

instead of what can be true.

OUTSTANDING OPTIMISM

The fourth superhero I would like to introduce you to is the Outstanding Optimism. I enjoy all the heroes, but Optimism may be one of my favorites. Optimism is like a leader of the superheroes because, when you think about it, mantras, affirmations, and compliments are all a form of optimism. It simultaneously draws its power from and builds up your inner strength. It can help you overcome just about any obstacle you face. There are times when it seems like everything is going wrong, but if you have even just a little optimism, you have the power to see your way out of what may seem like a bad situation.

Optimism is a mindset that relies on your ability to see the bright side of things. When people talk about the glass being half full instead of half empty, that is optimism—focusing on what is good about a situation instead of what is bad about it. Have you ever been around people who complain often? Does it seem like they always have something negative to say? That is because they choose not only to see the bad in the situation, but they choose to dwell on it.

If all you see is the negative, then it can be difficult to see anything else. The same is true for seeing the positive. If you are a person who constantly talks about the silver lining of a situation and can see the good in most cases, then your mind will become trained to that. Our brains are very powerful organs. They send signals to the rest of the body. Therefore, if we are constantly feeding it positive messages, it relays them throughout. A happy mind equals a happy body.

There is a science behind this idea. The brain releases "feel-good" chemicals to the body called endorphins. There are many ways to boost the release of endorphins. You can exercise, dance, make art, listen to music you love, laugh, think positively, and the list goes on. Endorphins can help to reduce stress, anxiety, and depression. So, now you know the science behind why some of your favorite activities put you in a better mood!

Life is full of bad luck, bad timing, and bad situations, but you must constantly remind yourself, and others, that there is good out there if we can just recognize it. From news headlines to social media posts, you don't have to look far to find bad news, which is why the world needs more people who thrive off hope. People who are willing to look at gray clouds and remind us, "The rain helps us grow."

Who would you rather be around—someone who is constantly complaining or negative, or someone who is hopeful and positive? Optimism is like a magnet. It attracts what it gives off. Others will feed off your energy. What could be more powerful than that?

Optimism can also help us handle some of the more mundane tasks we encounter. Think about something you do not like to do. Now think about why you do not like to do it. Let's just say it is . . . homework. If you look at the benefits of the task instead of the labor of it, it can make the execution of it less painful. More mastery, better grades, increased discipline: all benefits of doing the assignment that you are dreading. Or maybe you prefer to focus on the more immediate, in which case you can approach it as "After I finish my homework, I get to do X." Mindset is everything!

Someone may have even "made" you read this book, and you weren't looking forward to it. Instead of looking at it as a burden, think of it as an opportunity to learn new ways to use words. Or, when you have to eat vegetables, for those of you who don't enjoy a good brussels sprout. If all else fails, you can tell yourself, "This is the best way for me to get dessert."

There are things that I do not look forward to doing as an adult, but optimism has helped me push through those situations and look back and say, "That was not as bad as I was making it out to be." If you allow them, negative thoughts can make situations and even our perception of people far worse than what they are.

So, let's think about another activity that most kids don't look forward to—chores. Let's say that you don't like doing dishes and you dread when dinnertime is over because you know that means it's your time to get to work. Well, what if you changed your outlook on that small task. Instead of thinking about how it affects you, think about how it affects others. Sometimes, just changing the language you use to describe something can reset your attitude. Instead of saying "Doing the dishes is a chore," try "Doing the dishes is a responsibility." With just a simple word swap, you've now reframed it as a privilege to help your guardian who works and has provided that meal. You are contributing to their rest and giving them one less thing to think about, amid the many decisions they must make daily. Being able to provide that type of comfort is an honor, especially for the people you love. Looking at things from a different vantage point is an easy way to form an optimistic and positive mindset.

Words of Optimism List

- Awesome
- Beautiful (one of my favorites)
- Delightful
- Enjoyable
- Excellent
- Happy
- Impressive
- Jovial
- Lovely
- Magical
- Outstanding
- Promising
- Uplifting

super thoughts

What is something that you look forward to?

Think about a tough situation you've gone through. What was a positive that came from it?

CHALLENGE:
Go one day without complaining about anything.

WO

rds versus

NTMENTS

Defining Disappointment

I have been let down before,

> but I learned to keep my head high.

I have been let down before,

> but I learned to keep my standards high.

ONE OF THE MOST EXCITING THINGS ABOUT

being a human being with a mind and consciousness is that we can set goals and have dreams. We can aspire to be, and that is beautiful. But one of the downfalls of that same gift is that we can be disappointed if those dreams or goals do not materialize the way we saw them in our head.

Have you ever had a goal, or thought something was going to go a certain way and it did not? It can be something small, or big. Think about how you felt in the moment. I used to take disappointments hard. When I was younger, and playing sports, I would cry if I lost a big game, and I thought I could have done more. To be honest, I have cried as an adult after losing a big game that I was coaching because I wished I could have done more for my players. I have had career, relationship, and friendship disappointments. They do not stop once you become an adult, but the difference between adulthood and my younger self is how I perceived disappointments.

It is human nature to be disappointed, especially if you are a passionate person like me, but you do not have to be destroyed by it. You need to remind yourself that there are more opportunities to come—even if it is not the same opportunity, there will be others. You cannot measure yourself by the times you fell short, but by how many times you decided to move forward. After disappointment, do you keep climbing or do you sulk?

Don't get me wrong—there is nothing wrong with sulking. It is important to sit with how you feel, but it is also important to assess the most successful path forward. You cannot tear yourself or the world down because things did not go your way. When I am coaching, and my team loses a big game in the season,

I sit with my feelings regarding what just happened, then I immediately start planning for next season and thinking of ways to avoid those same pitfalls. That approach can be implemented for many things in life.

Let's say you failed a test. You have the right to be sad or frustrated about it, but your next moves should be thinking about what happened and planning for the next one. Did you study hard enough? Were you focused? Do you need extra help? The only way to get different results the next time is if you have an honest conversation about yourself. And it is also important to remember that some disappointments have nothing to do with you.

There will be times in life when other people will let you down. Sometimes they will let you down repeatedly. There may be times where adults promise to do things for you, like take you places or show up for you, and they don't come through. You may have friends who you expected to be loyal to you or look out for you, and they don't. Siblings can even be disappointing at times, for various reasons. You surely cannot blame yourself for moments like these. It is very easy to get into the mindset that you are the problem, but sometimes things just happen. The more you remind yourself of that, the less weight you put on disappointment.

Which is why it's important how you communicate your disappointment to others. Your language should always match the situation, to the best of your ability. (I am aware that we are all human and sometimes emotions get the best of us.) If your disappointment stems from an honest mistake or a small inconvenience, then your reaction should match the weight of the situation. Even if the disappointment is big, try to find language that represents how you feel without becoming heavy on someone else.

For instance, maybe in the heat of the moment, you say (or want to say), "I hate you!" when, in reality, you really mean, "I'm disappointed in you" or "You hurt my feelings" or "I'm frustrated." Or, suppose someone accidentally spills something on you. You may want to lash out and call them "stupid" or "clumsy," but you can just say, "I really liked this shirt and I'm upset that it's dirty now." You can declare feelings without being nasty about it.

Express yourself, let people know how you feel with clarity and efficiency, but do not make a spectacle of the situation. If you feel your emotions leading the way, then take a moment before starting the conversation, choose your words carefully, then come back to it. Sometimes we speak too fast without assessing our feelings. Your feelings may be compounded with other moments, and you do not want to take that out on people who do not deserve it. Always try your best to pinpoint where your disappointment is coming from and address it accordingly. And do not forget the secret sauce—grace.

Phrases to Use for Disappointment

- I was let down when you _____.
- It was disappointing when _____.
- Next time it would be better if you _____.
- I was really looking forward to _____, so if you could _____ in the future, that would be better.
- I know you probably tried your best, but that made me feel _____.

super thoughts

When was the last time you were disappointed?

How do you normally handle disappointment?

How do you handle when you have disappointed someone?

The Flight of Empathy

If I could take your pain,

fold it into paper planes

and release them

into the distant wind—

one by one—

I would.

But I can't.

So, I will listen,

and try to lift your spirits.

Make you feel lighter.

So, your smile can spread

just like the wings

of paper planes.

The fifth superhero I would like to introduce you to is the Enormous Empathy. What if I told you that you could transform? What if I told you that you could be a safe space? Well, that's Empathy's superpower. Empathy creates compassion and understanding in you in a way that makes others feel safe around you.

Empathy is being able to not just understand but to share in the feelings of others. Unlike sympathy, where you provide pity for someone's situation, but you don't necessarily place yourself in their situation to feel what they are feeling. So, when you are being empathetic you are not just listening to other people's stories, you are placing yourself in their shoes and trying your best to understand what they may be feeling or going through. The more empathy you present to the world, the more connected you are to other human beings. The more connected you are to other human beings, the bigger you become. People say it is a small world, but it is not. It is full of so many of us and we all have different experiences, and the more you connect yourself with the experiences of others, the more you grow as a person.

When you are in conversation with others and they are telling you a story, do not be quick to insert yourself or share your own anecdote; instead, ask them how certain parts of their experience made them feel. But be aware of how they respond. Do not try to force people to share beyond what they are comfortable sharing. All you can do is present the safe space; it is not your job to make them open up. Be genuine in not only your listening, but in your responses as well. For example, instead of saying "I know what you mean," try "Tell me more," "I hear you," or "Can you elaborate?" Giving people the space to expand on their feelings can be more helpful than you could imagine.

There are times, however, when your role shifts from listener to contributor. If you can relate to a feeling a person is going through, and the moment is right, let them know your story if you are comfortable sharing it. Shared vulnerability brings people closer, and it helps people feel less alone. You may not have been through the exact same situation as them, but you may have experienced the same emotions that they are going through, and that connection is important.

One of my favorite things to do with my family is to hear stories about their day. If my sons are telling me about something that happened at school, then I ask them how they reacted, how they felt about it, or why that stuck out to them. I am not with them every second of the day, so to get a glimpse of how their encounters affect them helps me understand them more and makes us closer. And the interesting thing that I have noticed about empathy is that it can be contagious.

Lately, my youngest son has been very adamant about asking people how they are feeling and if they are happy. This behavior brings a smile to my face because I see him growing bigger every time he does it. You would be surprised how often people go through life without people genuinely caring about their well-being. We often ask each other "How is it going?" as a casual greeting, but we rarely care about the real answer.

We all deserve to be cared about, to be seen, to have someone understand us to the best of their ability. There is so much apathy in the world, and it can be easy to become desensitized to other people's lives. As a villain, apathy can be defeated with words that show that you care, understand, and have interest in others. "I am here for you," "I know it must be hard going through that," and "I can relate to that" are all expressions that can help defeat apathy. Be present and make people feel worthy of your attention.

Phrases for Empathy

- I understand how you feel.
- I can see why you are angry.
- That makes sense to me.
- I would feel the same way!
- I would be disappointed, too.
- I can understand why that hurt your feelings.
- I understand your perspective.
- I admire how you handled that.
- Wow, that sounds scary.
- I probably would've reacted the same way.

super thoughts

What type of listener are you?

Would you be able to empathize with someone who isn't your friend?

When was the last time someone showed you empathy?

rds

versus

URES*

Lessons in Failing

I was told

we are measured

by how many times

we choose to get up

after we have fallen.

I choose to believe

I am measured

by how many things

I have learned

after I have failed.

BY NOW, YOU SHOULD NOTICE

a pattern in how language can be used to help us overcome challenges. If you start with acknowledging what's in front of you while showing grace to yourself and others, then you've taken the first steps to reframing the situation or mindset. That rule applies for when you fail, too. Now, remember: Failure is different from a mistake. You can make a mistake and still succeed at something.* You can put too much flour in a cake batter, but if you increase the rest of the ingredients, you can still make a lovely cake (with some batter left over to make cupcakes)— that's a mistake. But if you leave the cake in for too long, then you burn it and fail at making a digestible cake. Failure is more definitive than mistakes, but although mistakes can lead to failure, failure isn't final.

Let me explain this another way. You can fail repeatedly, but that *does not* mean you are a failure. If anything, that means that you are a trier. One of the most dangerous things you can do when you fail is tell yourself that you were not "meant" to do the thing you failed at. What you *are* meant to do is learn from your failures. Take the baking example, for instance. If you left the cake in too long, that doesn't mean you weren't meant to bake; it means you need to adjust your timer next time. There's a big difference between "I can't bake" and "I need to pay more attention when I'm baking." One implies defeat, while the other leaves room for growth and success.

How you communicate with yourself after a failure can be the difference between you succeeding in future attempts and the pitfall of believing you are not good enough and giving up. One of the biggest reasons that failure affects us so much is because of pride. As human beings, we often worry too much about

* Please note that you can fail at something and still eventually succeed at it.

how we look to others. If you fall off your bike and no one is around, it is easier to get back on your bike and try again, because you are the only one dealing with your perception of you. It is when we fall in front of others that the fear of judgment and ridicule makes the weight of failure feel too heavy to bear.

You also must be careful to not take on other people's expectations of you and consider it failure when you fall short of it. If you know that you did your best but did not do as well as someone else wanted you to do, that is not failure. You must be able to tell the difference between the two or you will walk around carrying other peoples' versions of you on your back. It may take you seven times to get something right, when someone thought it should only take you three. If you stopped after that third time because their perception of you made you think you were not good enough, then you would have never known that seven was your magic number. Exist on your own rubric, while still staying open to advice and constructive criticism. We all succeed at different paces.

So, how do you overcome the paralyzing fear of judgment? You tell yourself that your sense of self is the one that matters, and you keep saying that until you believe it. People who can fail in front of others and keep going are some of the most mentally tough people who exist. When you get to the point where you see the lesson in your failure and not the embarrassment, that is maturity.

However, that said, the lesson you learn in one instance will not necessarily ensure success the next time around. Life is not like the movies. Just because you try again does not mean it will magically be the outcome you set out for in the beginning. Life is a series of attempts and refinement. I have failed many times. I have set out to do things that didn't work out and required that I keep tweaking my approach and execution. The learning never stops.

Be kind to yourself in these moments. The world is cruel enough. You do not need to add to that weight. Tell yourself all the things you learned from your failure and how proud of yourself you are for trying. If you fail a test, instead of saying "I'm dumb" or "I suck at math," try "I need to study harder (or more)." Or if you miss an important shot in a game, instead of saying "I'm not good enough," try "Even the pros miss shots from time to time. I'll keep practicing." See your failures as challenges, not as stop signs.

Also, we can't forget that we aren't the only ones who deal with failure. Being a good friend can also mean being a good cheerleader. Our friends and family also deal with failure, so, at times, we are going to have to find words to help them through those tough times. Simple things like "I know you've been working hard, and I'm rooting for you" or "Your teammates are lucky to have someone like you on their side" can help those close to you get over a failure that they are dealing with.

It's often easier to say positives things to others than it is to say them to ourselves; that is why I spent so much time detailing how important it is to speak success into our own lives. But never forget how much others need to hear those words as well.

super thoughts

When was the last time you failed?

Does failing stop you from trying again?

What are some of the best lessons you've learned from failing?

Glorious Gratitude

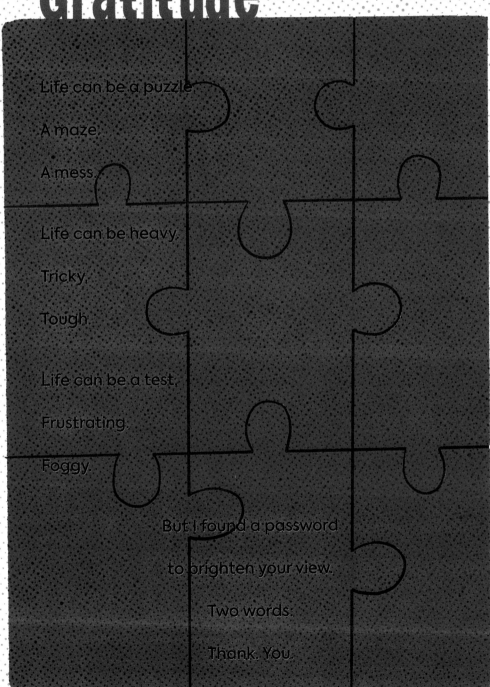

Life can be a puzzle.

A maze.

A mess.

Life can be heavy.

Tricky.

Tough.

Life can be a test.

Frustrating.

Foggy.

But I found a password

to brighten your view.

Two words:

Thank. You.

GLORIOUS GRATITUDE

It's only fitting that the final superhero I introduce you to is one of my all-time favorites—the Glorious Gratitude. In a similar way to how Affirmation has the power to control your mind, Gratitude has the power to control hearts.

Naming the things we are grateful for helps us see those things more clearly on a daily basis. One of my favorite things to do is start and end my day with a list of things I am grateful for. I try to be as intentional and mindful as possible about those things. I say thank you for things big and small. Love, time, family, and friends are things I always mention. I am so grateful for the time I get to spend with the people I love, and the time I get to spend doing the things I love. How amazing that is. I have noticed that the more I name the things I am grateful for, the clearer they are to me.

It's also important to include gratitude for our failures. That's right. It may sound weird to think of failure as something to be grateful for, but if we can look to the lessons we learn after each setback, then we can better appreciate the range of experiences we have in life. If we are never faced with failure, then we never have to push ourselves outside our comfort zones. We never know what we're truly capable of. And that's part of the beauty of life. We sometimes get second (and third and fourth) chances. We should hold gratitude for each one because they serve as an opportunity to better ourselves. To better the world around us.

Life moves so fast, and we can miss so much if we forget to be grateful for the moments. Take the time to look out the window on your ride home from school, really listen to your friend's story, look at the colors you are surrounded by, pay attention to things that made you smile or laugh throughout the day. Call those things by name before you go to sleep.

Gratitude is something to be shared, which is why it's important to tell the people in your life how much you appreciate them. Watch how they react. We should always remain mindful that none of life's joys are promised to us. We all see stories every day about tragedies and unforeseen incidents. Most people do not wake up expecting anything like that to happen, but sometimes they do. So, because life is so unpredictable, we must be grateful for the small wonders we are gifted each day. When you are intentional about your gratitude, those things that you appreciate show up more frequently.

Being grateful helps us see the beauty in the world. It is so easy to get caught up in the bad news we see so often, but gratitude creates optimism. If we experience good and can call it by its name, then it is easier for us to believe that good exists in the world, even when we are told it is hard to find. It is not. We are surrounded by it. A lot of times, we are the good things we are looking for. Be grateful for yourself as well.

I recommend you create a journal to keep track of what you are grateful for daily. On days when it is hard to think of anything, it can be nice to be able to go back and look at the days when you had much to appreciate. It is a beautiful reminder. And while it is okay to be grateful for material things, I challenge you to find as many things as possible that did not cost a thing to put on that list. I told you early on that this book is just as much about human connection as it is about anything, and those things that bring us together as humans are equally as important as, if not more than, the things we spend our money on.

Being grateful can be contagious as well, similar to optimism. Pay attention to the people who complain the most around you. Start naming things that you are grateful for, in an organic way, and watch how they start to complain less, and, in some instances, you may notice them starting to call out things they are grateful for after a while. We are all somebody's lighthouse. You never know the influence you have on others. Shine your light, and watch others do the same.

Gratitude is not exclusively to make you feel good, it also makes others hopeful about extending themselves. When someone does something nice for you and you show genuine gratitude, it can fulfill them; and inspire them to not only do for you, but for others too. To be appreciated can be comforting, and that can become contagious. So, as much as you are helping yourself, you are helping others as well.

*Write a handwritten letter of gratitude
to someone who wouldn't expect it from you.*

*What are some things that
you are grateful for about yourself?*

CHALLENGE:
Make a list of things you are grateful for
(make this a daily habit if you can).

AUTHOR'S NOTE

I am grateful that this book found its way to you. I am even more grateful that you stayed until the end. That is a big deal to me. You are one of my good things. I am grateful for *you*.

This book is about you and all the strength you embody. I wanted to show you the power of language, how you have a slew of superheroes ready to help whenever you feel you need it. But the truth is, those super-heroes exist within you already. You have the power to affirm and make people feel larger than life with your compliments. You have the ability to slow down time with your mantras or change perspectives with your optimism. You can transform into a safe space through empathy and change hearts with gratitude.

YOU are the hero. Now I leave it to you to live a thankful life.

ACKNOWLEDGMENTS

Every child, even the ones at heart, who read this book, thank you for giving me a chance.

Every parent who made their child read this, or recommended it to someone else, you make the world go round.

My wonderful editor, Allison Cohen, and everyone at Running Press Kids, thank you for believing in me.

My amazing friend and literary agent, Lilly Ghahremani, thank you for always having your pom-poms ready.

Zaire, Zulu, Cassandra, and Elizabeth, thank you for being muses for this book without knowing it.

ABOUT THE AUTHOR

Harold Green is an ever-evolving artist whose vibrant storytelling and passionate, lyrical delivery captivate audiences domestically and internationally. Using poetry as his central art form, Green is a highly sought-after speaker, bandleader, and event producer. His first collection of poetry, *From Englewood, with Love, 2014*, earned the prestigious Carl Sandburg Literary Award. He is also the author of *Black Roses* and *Black Oak*, a duo of illustrated volumes inspired by his viral odes to Black celebrities who are making history today, as well as *The Rainbow Park* and *The Numbers Store*, the first two books in the Sunday Adventures board book series, and the picture book *Love Bubble*.

Green studied English Secondary Education at Grambling State University before earning a Bachelor of Arts in Creative Writing from DePaul University and a Master of Humanities in Creative Writing from Tiffin University. Green specializes in making poetry an accessible art form for all. His performances have been featured at festivals, rallies, and colleges across the country, and he is the architect and curator of "Flowers for the Living," an artist collective that layers poetry on performances by Chicago's top singers and musicians. He has created numerous recorded albums of poetry, videos, plays, and other productions. Green has been featured in the *New York Times*, *Chicago Tribune*, *Chicago Sun-Times*, *Ebony Web*, *Windy City Live*, and *CBS Chicago*, among others.

He is a proud son, brother, husband, father, teacher, coach, and mentor.

ABOUT THE ILLUSTRATOR

Andrea Pippins is an illustrator and author who has a passion for creating images that reflect what she wants to see in art, media, and design. Her work has been featured in *Essence Magazine*, the *New York Times*, and *O: The Oprah Magazine*. She has produced artwork for brands such as ESPN, Five Below, Instagram, Sephora, Lincoln Center for the Performing Arts, Malala Fund, Nick Jr., USPS, and VH1.

Pippins is the author of *Who Will You Be?*, a look into the life of a little boy and the people in his community who shape who he is; *Becoming Me*, an interactive journal for young women to color, doodle, and brainstorm their way to a creative life; and *We Inspire Me*, a collection of essays, interviews, and advice on cultivating and empowering one's own creative community. She also illustrated *Young, Gifted and Black*; *Step Into Your Power*; and *Big Ideas for Young Thinkers*.

Pippins is based in Stockholm.